© MCMXCIX by Barbour Publishing, Inc.

ISBN 1-58660-648-6

Cover image © Adobe Studios

Published by Humble Creek, P.O. Box 719, Uhrichsville, Ohio 44683

Printed in China.
5 4 3

Christmas at Home
HOLIDAY
PARTY PLANNER

Compiled by
Ellyn Sanna

HUMBLECREEK
INSPIRATION FOR LIFE

Be joyful at your Feast.

DEUTERONOMY 16:14

For unto us a child is born,
to us a son is given. . . .
And he will be called. . .
Prince of Peace.

ISAIAH 9:6

The holidays are here again—that joyous, hectic season of parties and get-togethers. As we plan our holiday parties, let's not lose sight of the season's meaning and wonder: We are celebrating the birthday of the Prince of Peace. So give yourself plenty of time to prepare for a fun-filled celebration, and as you make your plans, let the Prince of Peace reign in your heart.

> _"**A** certain man was preparing a_
> _great banquet and invited many guests. . . ._
> _Then the master told his servant,_
> _'Go out to the road and country lanes_
> _and make them come in,_
> _so that my house will be full.'"_
>
> LUKE 14:16, 23

First Things First

__ Set the time and date for the party.

_____

_____

_____

__ Decide on a realistic budget.

_____

_____

_____

__ Prepare the guest list.

In arriving at the time and place for your party, try to arrange a time that will be convenient for most of your guests. For example, a Friday or Saturday night works out best for most people; try to set the time for the party late enough so people can arrive on time without rushing—perhaps by 7:00 P.M.

Before you go any further with your party plans, you need to establish how much you can afford to spend on this party, both in time and money. A holiday celebration doesn't need to be extravagant to be successful, so be careful not to overextend yourself. Remember, your goal should not be to impress, but rather to share with others the Christ Child's love and joy. During this busy and expensive season, we need to keep our focus on Him.

So if your budget is limited, here are some ideas that will help keep your party from consuming too much time or money:

— Host a "potluck" party. (Ask each guest to bring a different course of the meal.)

_____

_____

_____

_____

_____

_____

_____

_____

— Organize a "progressive party." (Each host provides one course and the guests move from home to home.)

— Give a single-course party (for example, a dessert party or an hors d'oeuvres party).

Given the limits of your budget, how many guests you wish to invite depends on whether you plan a seated meal or a buffet dinner. For a sit-down dinner, eight people or fewer usually work out best. But if you plan to serve buffet style, you may be able to serve twenty-five to thirty people. You'll need to consider how many people will be able to comfortably fit in your home. If you want a gathering that's larger than your home can accommodate, here are some other possible locations:

— church halls
— apartment complex
    party rooms
— restaurants

— clubhouses
— motel or hotel party rooms
— VFW or American Legion
    halls

As you decide on the size of your party, keep in mind your objective for having this particular gathering. If you want an informal, intimate get-together, then you should keep your guest list short. If your goal is a more formal party, then you could go for a longer list. But don't feel you should repay all of your social obligations in one grand swoop.

As you make up your guest list, remember that hospitality is an important biblical ministry. As Christians, we don't need to be preoccupied with impressing our friends, relatives, and associates; instead, we can use this as a time to share our love with others, particularly those who may be lonely and forgotten during this special season.

Scents of the Holidays

Combine in a small saucepan:

peelings from 2 oranges
3 cinnamon sticks (crushed)
6 whole cloves (crushed)

3 whole allspice
3 cups water

Bring to a boil, then reduce heat and simmer continuously during the day before your party to create a welcoming Christmas aroma.

An even easier way to achieve the same effect is to sprinkle ground cinnamon on the burners of an electric stove, which will fill the air with a Christmasy fragrance. This fragrant trick began in the days of Solomon, when cinnamon was burned to perfume the air inside the temple.

ELLYN SANNA, *New York*

*O*ffer hospitality to one another
without grumbling.

1 PETER 4:9

Four to six weeks before your party:

___ Decide on a theme and decorations.

> XMAS on main St 2010
> FRi 26 → 5⁴⁵ pm Parade to tree lighting
> SAT 27 → 4-6 arts center wreath auction
>   wino tasting
> SUN 28
> Horsey ride, Mrs claus, CandyLAND
> Live Reindeer, Light PARADE
> TREE Lighting
> NORTH Pole lobby of Fnye Motel
> WWW.aDIRONDACKchristMASonMAinStreet.coM
>   WWWOLDFORGENY.COM

___ Make or buy the invitations.

___ Make or buy decorations.

The most obvious theme for your holiday party is Christmas itself, the birthday of our Lord. So take advantage of your Christmas decorations and incorporate them into your party decorations. Be sure to have a nativity scene on a table or a mantel. You can also place a Bible open to the second chapter of Luke (the story of Christ's birth) on a coffee table or other small table. Here are some other ideas for a party theme that will tie in with Christmas:

— toys (for example, teddy bears, china dolls or rag dolls, antique toys—these can be displayed around your home as centerpieces, perched on stairs, lined up on mantles, or placed in a circle around your tree)

— international Christmas customs—or your own ethnic background's traditional Christmas. For example:

* In Mexico brightly colored nativity figures and papier-mâché objects are used for decorations, as well as piñatas.
* An empty chair is left at the table of Czech feasts to remind guests of the Christ Child's spiritual presence.
* The Swiss make tree ornaments of bright tissue figures with chocolates hidden inside.

* Scandinavians use straw and wheat in their decorations. Sheaves of grain are also put on poles outside for the birds' Christmas feast.
* Japanese decorate with pastel paper fans and origami figures.
* Germans hang an Advent wreath from the ceiling with bright red ribbons. They decorate with delicate blown-glass ornaments—and trays of cookies!

— color themes (you don't have to limit yourself to the traditional red and green; instead, consider gold and silver, blue and white, or burgundy)

— Christmas past (antiques of all sorts—check out your parents' or grandparents' attic)

Decorations

As you plan your party's decorations, you might decide to order fresh flowers from your florist for a centerpiece or other decorations, but you can also plan to decorate more cheaply with things like:

— baskets filled with pinecones, evergreen, or apples
— ribbons and garland
— wreaths made from almost anything:
  * evergreen branches
  * pinecones
  * dried herbs
  * dried apple or orange slices
  * grapevines
  * holly
  * dried flowers
  * cloth braids
  * braided breads

- Christmas trees of all sorts:
  * Styrofoam cones can be covered with candies, nuts, cones, or cookies using a glue gun.
  * live trees
  * quilted trees
  * tiered party dishes with red and gold ribbons or candles

- strings of colored or white lights (your home's everyday decorations will look Christmasy when strung with tiny white lights)
- paper snowflakes
- candles of all sorts
- poinsettias
- gingerbread men and houses
- luminaries for outside your house
  * paper bag (lunch size) luminaries: Use a paper punch to make a design, then fold the top of each bag down about one inch and add about two inches of sand. Put a votive candle in the center of the sand, making sure it doesn't touch the edges of the bag. Light the candle and place bags two or three feet apart along the edge of your steps,

*S*hare with God's people. . . .
Practice hospitality.

ROMANS 12:13

Three weeks before your party:

_   Send out invitations.
_   Plan menu and activities.

_____

_____

_____

_____

_____

_   Think about gifts to give to your guests.

_____

_____

_____

_____

_____

___ Decide what music (if any) you'll use.

_____

_____

_____

_____

_____

After the invitations are sent, you need to decide on your menu. You may want your menu to be in keeping with your party's theme. (For instance, if your theme was an international or ethnic Christmas, you might want to have each course represent a different nationality or have the entire meal follow a particular ethnic tradition.) Whatever you serve, though, simplicity is the key word! After all, the Christmas season can become hectic enough without creating unnecessary grief for yourself. Keep in mind that the more items you can prepare the day ahead, the less frustrating dinnertime will be.

Following are four menu suggestions.

Menu #1
(good for a buffet-style meal)

Beef stroganoff
Mixed vegetable casserole
Bran muffins
Christmas ambrosia
Coffee, tea

Menu #2
(nice for a seated dinner)

Baked chicken
Yam casserole
Cranberry salad
Brown 'n' serve rolls
Funnel cake
Coffee, tea

Menu #3
(good for a buffet-style meal)

Spaghetti and meatballs
Tossed green salad
Italian cheese bread
Ice cream with strawberries
Coffee, tea

Menu #4
(good for either a buffet or seated meal)

Honey-baked ham
Scalloped potatoes
Asparagus spears
Salad
Buttermilk biscuits
Carrot cake
Coffee, tea

You may want to plan games for your get-together that will tie in with your party's theme. For instance, if your theme is Christmas Past, then you might want to play some old-fashioned games like blindman's buff or charades; if you were having a Mexican party, you would want to have breaking a piñata as part of your entertainment, etc. Or if your guests don't all know each other, you may want to have a "mixer" game in mind to help break the ice. (Your library will have books that can give you ideas for party games.) But if you and your guests all know each other well, you may not need to plan any extra activity. Instead, you might want to simply sing Christmas carols, read the Christmas story from the Bible out loud, and share Christmas memories from your childhood.

Since this is the gift-giving season, you could send a small gift home with each of your guests (although this is certainly not necessary). Or you may want to have prizes for the games you play. A Christmas ornament for each guest is one simple and easy solution. Another idea is to have English "crackers" for each guest. When the crackers are snapped, they reveal a small gift. (Crackers are available from specialty catalogs and can be reused year after year.) Here are some other inexpensive suggestions:

— a decorative tin filled with homemade cookies or candy (or if you don't have time to make anything, holiday-wrapped Hershey Kisses or red and green M&Ms are just as nice)
— molded cheeseballs
— decorative containers filled with pasta
— homemade dressings or vinegars in decorative bottles
— baskets of spices, teas, coffee beans, or nuts
— bags or baskets of fresh fruit
— jars of homemade jam or jelly
— coffee cakes
— selections of your favorite recipes
— homemade Christmas stockings (if you sew, you can use left-over scraps for these inexpensive gifts—but they'll be time-consuming)
— baskets of muffins
— loaves of homemade bread
— containers of homemade fudge

— oatmeal containers, milk cartons, or shoe boxes covered with holiday wrapping paper
— strawberry baskets
— coffee mugs
— bread pans
— clay flowerpots
— brown paper sacks
— jelly jars
— mason jars
— margarine or whipped topping containers decorated with spray paint and stickers. Any of these containers can be easily filled by using melted chocolate to coat:
  * pretzels
  * raisins
  * caramels
  * animal crackers
  * Oreos
  * nuts
  * Chinese noodles
  * marshmallows

*W*hether or not you decide to give gifts to your guests, a holiday party needs music. As your guests arrive, you could have some type of Christmas music playing softly on the stereo. It needs to be light so as to create a mood and not detract from conversation. If you have an ethnic theme for your party, music will help to heighten the atmosphere. Look through your music collection for a suitable selection, or borrow from your friends or your local library.

*"When you give a luncheon or dinner. . .
invite [those in need],
and you will be blessed."*

LUKE 14:12–14

Two weeks before your party:

__ Prepare a shopping list.

_____

_____

_____

__ Order any arrangements/material from the florist or locate
(borrow, buy, or hunt down in your house) the decorations
you'll be using.

_____

_____

_____

___ Buy or collect material to make gifts.

_____

_____

_____

___ Check to see that you have all the necessary serving dishes, utensils, tablecloths, and napkins on hand. Arrange to borrow (or buy if your budget allows) the things you're lacking.

_____

_____

_____

___ Plan how you will welcome your guests (with crackers and cheese, music, a warm-up game, a warm drink, or a glass of punch).

_____

_____

_____

Beverages

— Fill ice trays with lemonade and freeze. Use cubes in punch or apple cider.
— Freeze strawberries in Christmas molds and float in punch.
— Add orange slices, cinnamon sticks, and cloves to hot cider.
— Put floating cloved oranges in hot cranberry juice cocktail punch.
— Combine coffee and cocoa to make mocha-cocoa.
— Make Russian tea from Tang, tea, cinnamon, and cloves.
— Make Mexican cocoa from hot chocolate mix and cinnamon.

*And do not forget to do good and
to share with others,
for with such sacrifices God is pleased.*

HEBREWS 13:16

One week before your party:

__ Make a head count of guests who will be attending.

_____

_____

_____

__ Clean your house (any big jobs that need to be done).

_____

_____

_____

__ Make sure all decorating material, gifts, menu ingredients, etc. will be available for your party.

_____

_____

_____

__ Begin decorating your house.

_____

_____

_____

__ Begin shopping for menu ingredients.

_____

_____

_____

___ Do a final head count of the guest list. If you need to fill in any cancellations, you might want to ask God to direct you to someone you might not have thought of, someone who particularly needs the ministry of hospitality during this holiday season.

_____

_____

_____

$\mathcal{P}$lay Christmas music as you make your preparations. As you work, prayerfully meditate on the fact that you are preparing a birthday celebration for the Baby Jesus.

Christmas Snow
(for window decorating)

$\frac{1}{2}$ cup lukewarm water
$\frac{1}{2}$ cup plus about 2 slightly rounded
T. mild soap flakes or granules
assorted doilies or homemade snowflakes

Combine the water and soap flakes in a mixing bowl. When the soap is dissolved, beat with an electric mixer until it looks like stiff meringue. Tape paper doilies or snowflakes to the inside of the window and use a sponge to dab the whipped mixture over the perforations. Remove the doily immediately and allow the design to dry. (After the holidays, simply wipe off with window cleaner and a soft cloth.)

TAMMY CAREY, *Pennsylvania*

Keep on loving each other. . . .
Do not forget to entertain strangers,
for by so doing some people have
entertained angels without knowing it.

HEBREWS 13:1–2

The day before your party:

___ If you'll be taking pictures, make sure you have film.
___ Pick up any flowers, etc. from the florist.
___ Clean bathrooms; vacuum and dust any rooms that will be used during the party.
___ Wrap gifts (or prepare baskets or containers).

_ Do any last-minute shopping for the menu.

———————————————————————————————

———————————————————————————————

———————————————————————————————

_ Put finishing touches on your decorations.

———————————————————————————————

———————————————————————————————

———————————————————————————————

_ Make sure your music is ready to go.

———————————————————————————————

———————————————————————————————

———————————————————————————————

__ Prepare any dishes that can be made ahead.

_____

_____

_____

__ Plan timetable for cooking foods so that everything will
be ready at the same time.

_____

_____

_____

$\mathcal{P}$erhaps the most important last-minute preparation you can make is to allow yourself some time to relax and enjoy the Christmas season. Remember, Jesus loved you enough to be born as a human baby. That amazing fact should help you keep in perspective all the many things you have to do.

The day of your party:

__ Touch up your house and decorations.

_____

_____

_____

__ Chill whatever needs it.

_____

_____

_____

Phone charger
Pills
computer/charger chord
tooth Fixer
Anacids
COLD MED/CHZZ